# Dealing with Mental Illness Depression and Bipolar Disorder

mental illness

Leo Hardy

Published by cannon books and media, 2017.

DEALING WITH MENTAL ILLNESS DEPRESSION AND BIPOLAR DISORDER

**First edition. April 20, 2017.**



Written by Leo Hardy.

DEALING WITH MENTAL ILLNESS
THE COLLECTION PART 1
DEPRESSION AND BIPOLAR DISORDER
Edited by

Rodney Cannon

BOOK ONE
BIPOLAR DISORDER
DEALING WITH BIPOLAR DISORDER
By.
Leo Hardy

# CHAPTER ONE WHAT IS BIPOLAR DISORDER

*-So when I was 24, someone suggested to me that I was bipolar, and I thought that was ridiculous. I just thought he was trying to get out of treating me. But he was also responding to the chaotic nature of my life.- Carrie Fisher*

Bipolar Disorder also known as manic depression is a psychological disorder that makes the affected individual possess great mood shifts that usually affects their day to day tasks. Bipolar disorder symptoms often focus on mood and behavioral changes.

When you are feeling down, you may suffer a loss of interest in specific activities and switch from the rest of the world. When your moods shift to the other side, you may appear ecstatic and full of energy. The different mood swings can alter from time to time. They can happen only a few times or several times. In certain circumstances, bipolar and manic depression signs a can occur concurrently.

Despite bipolar disorder being a challenging and long-term health concern, you can continuously keep a guard on mood swings by devising an effective treatment plan. Most of the time, bipolar disorders can be easily controlled with the help of medications and psychotherapy.

Types of Bipolar Disorders:

Bipolar disorder is specified into categories each having a different set of symptoms:

•Bipolar disorder 1: Mood swings are associated with bipolar 1 disorder and can cause an immense loss of relationships, jobs and studies. Freaking attacks can be extreme and dangerous.

•Bipolar disorder 2: As compared to bipolar 1 disorder, bipolar 2 disorder is less severe. You can occasionally suffer from frustration, irritability but mainly you can carry on your day-to-day activities without much of a hassle. Instead of suffering from extreme mania, you suffer from hypomania, which is a less severe form of mania. In this disorder, duration of depression lasts longer than the duration of hypomania.

•Cyclothymic disorder: Cyclothymic disorder is a lighter form of bipolar disorder. With cyclothymia, depression and hypomania can be troublesome, but mood swings are manageable as they are with other types bipolar disorders.

•Not Specified - this is a treatable ailment and the signs presented by the patient don't occur in either of the three categories stated; the disorder varies from one person to another.

Symptoms of Bipolar Disorder:

Symptoms that arise are usually divided into depression and mania. The precise symptoms of bipolar disorder differ from individual to individual. For some people, depression can cause many worries while in other individuals, maniac situations are major problems. Symptoms of hypomania and depression can occur together, which is know as a mixed episode.

Signs that Manic Phase show:

1. Poor judgment. 2. Fast speech. 3. Behavior becomes aggressive. 4. Frequent altercations. 5. Decreased sleep. 6. Use of drugs or alcohol. 7. Regular absence from work.8. Frustration. 9. Reduced performance at work.

Symptoms of the depression phase:

1. Sleep issues. 2. Tiredness. 3. Despair. 4. Difficulty in concentration. 5. Low appetite. 6. Feeling cut out from the world. 7. Anxiety problems.

Causes:

The precise cause of bipolar disorder is still unknown. However, certain factors are believed to be associated with the disease:

•Patients with the bipolar disease tend to develop physical changes in the brain. How these changes happen and why they appear, is unsure.

•Unevenness in the brain chemicals plays a significant role in causing bipolar disorder and other mood disorders.

•Hormonal imbalance is also attributed to bipolar disorder.

•Bipolar disorder is seen more in people who have inherited this disease from a sibling or parent.

Risk Factors:

Factors that may increase the development of bipolar disorder are:

•Someone in the relation carrying the bipolar disorder gene.

•Taking high levels of stress.

•Inadequate drug intake.

•Early age, especially early 20s.

When to see a psychiatrist:

When you start experiencing symptoms of depression, stress or hypomania, see your therapist immediately. Bipolar disorder does not heal itself. Getting help from a medical service provider will do a great deal with managing your symptoms.

Treatment usually involves a mixture of therapy and medication treatment. Antidepressants, mood stabilizers, and anti-anxiety prescriptions are the prescribed medications. Treatment for adolescent bipolar usually lasts for years and may be taken into adulthood as well. However, the duration of the treatment is not the primary concern here. Rather, patients should focus on using their medication as the foundation for living a normal life with the least amount of problems coming from the condition. This case applies to both adolescents and adults.

Active bipolar disorder treatment can help manage the symptoms of the disease even though there is no cure for bipolar disorder. This disorder treatment often includes medication, therapy, and lifestyle maintenance to manage this complex condition.

Medication is perhaps the most important part of bipolar disorder treatment though many people including bipolar disorder patients do not take full advantage of the prescription that is available. A psychiatrist often prescribes a stabilizing mood medication. However, bipolar disorder patients are notoriously inconsistent with taking their medication.

In addition to medication, psychotherapy is often recommended for bipolar disorder treatment. Therapy does not necessarily treat the bipolar disorder directly, but helps the individual cope with the symptoms and can help the person to learn to manage stress so as to reduce the bipolar disorder symptoms.

Relationships often suffer from bipolar disorder and its symptoms. Part of the treatment for bipolar disorder can include family therapy, marriage counseling, or family sessions with the person's therapist to help strengthen the relationships and educate everyone on the effects of bipolar disorder.

Lifestyle management and regulation of self-care and habits are a common component of effective bipolar disorder treatment. It is strongly suggested that people with bipolar disorder maintain a regular sleep schedule and have a regular schedule of exercise and relaxation or stress management.

The general public has a lot of misconceptions about bipolar disorder. Therefore, the patient should educate themselves about bipolar disorder, its symptoms, and effective treatments. People with bipolar disorder may also have to educate their families and friends about the real nature of the condition as opposed to the extreme cases of the unmanaged bipolar disorder that they may have heard in the media.

An important part of bipolar treatment is emotional support from friends and family. Not all bipolar disorder patients have supportive friends and families. If the patient has a lack of emotional support, they can seek support from stable resources such as support groups for bipolar disorder and depression.

# CHAPTER TWO BIPOLAR AND THE FAMOUS

*- I'm fine, but I'm bipolar. I'm on seven medications, and I take medication three times a day. This constantly puts me in touch with the illness I have. I'm never quite allowed to be free of that for a day. It's like being a diabetic.- Carrie Fisher*

Photo provided by Alan Light

Bipolar depression and famous people normally aren't in the same sentence. Yet, it should be, since it's as common as Robin Leach's wine and dinner outings with his wife in Las Vegas. It's common in Hollywood as well as across the globe where celebrities reside. The subject matter of bipolar disorder and depression are among the most least talked about in public and sometimes considered a taboo word when it comes to family members much less celebrities.

It's so underrepresented in the medical field that more celebrities should talk openly about it; as Mel Gibson and Robert Downey, Jr. have done so in the past. It should be part of the treatment due to their constant limelight in the press. With medical disorders and film, it's amazing that it even is discussed besides being part of many discussions and shows due to Oprah's network and maybe even the Hallmark channel and Lifetime network.

With that said, there are some symptoms that people should be aware of when wanting to learn more about the two. First of all, symptoms of bipolar disorder include mania, emotional and physical, depressed moods, decreased self-confidence, self-worth and the loss of motivation. This includes no motive to make goals, go to work, and, basically, life in general. There's always that lingering sadness that comes over a person with bipolar depression. This is hard when it's a loved one, such as a spouse, a sibling or a parent. The best that can be done is seeking medical help and medication along with a strong support group and continuous activities.

For those who can't, some do admit to having bipolar

With celebrities, bipolar disorder and depressive people attempt to "fix" themselves by self medication such as Amy Winehouse, Kurt Cobain, Robert Downey, Jr., and Mel Gibson. Medical experts suggest that if they would have sought medical advice and attention, including psychiatric help and counseling, it could well have begin a medical regimen that saves lives to this day.

Unfortunately, it was too late for Cobain and Winehouse, RIP, which were prime examples of self-medication. It's the lack of admittance or knowledge of the disorders that cause many years of self medicated drug use for Downey, including imprisonment, today. He's overcome it and openly discusses it. Consequently, he's been told that he's the "poster child" for the self-medicated and bipolar disorder patients with the illness. Currently, he's doing well today, or so he's still saying he's not depressed, manic, or has bipolar. Yet, only time will tell; the sad thing is, no one wants to put a label on themselves or have a label put on them by any public press, friend, family member, or doctor when he/she doesn't really know how one really feels inside. (Read more: Downey, Jr. https://www.verywell.com/robert-downey-jr-actor-3796007 , Sept. 2016)

As for Mel Gibson, he's currently working on his disorder, as he did confess to having bipolar in 2008. Given with that confession, it made everyone realize that it had a major effect and partially to blame for all the mood swings, those frequent outbursts, and many issues that piled up on him while he was at his peak in Hollywood. Gibson had episodes that went viral, landed him in jail, and even banned him from certain events which if he wouldn't have had if he had seen a physician. Due to that fact, it may have prevented him from being "hated" on in certain parts of the world, respectively. It actually overshadowed his career, especially when he had just made a movie "The Passion of the Christ". He is still recovering from all this negative attention because of his denial or ignorance to the subject matter. He's had a positive light on him, yet is still working on this. In other words, turning away from his actual truth of having bipolar disorder will only make it worse for him and his career.

Since there are many celebrities with the disorder, maybe it would be a good thing to see "who's who" in celebrities or famous people that suffer from bipolar disorder, living or dead.

There are a number of Hollywood actors also who've suffered from bipolar disorders and depression. Among the many are Elizabeth Taylor and Patty Duke, and even Carrie Fisher, whom upon writing this article past in the morning on December, 27 2016, due to a heart attack. (Read more: http://www.msn.com/en-us/movies/celebrity/iconic-star-wars-actress-carrie-fisher-dies-at-60/ar-BBxCEWv?OCID=ansmsnnews11)

Other celebrities and well-known people with the disorders; depression/bipolar

In addition to the mentioned above, there are countless other celebrities who are said to have had or have bipolar disorder as well as depression. They are Drew Carey, Stephen Fry, Ozzy Osbourne, Ludwig Van Beethoven, Marilyn Monroe, Frank Sinatra, singers Axl Rose and Sinead O'Connor, writer Virginia Wolf, Lincoln's wife, Mary Todd Lincoln, ...and many many more.

In fact, even tough guys such as professional boxer, Mike Tyson, and actor Jean-Claude Van Damme suffered from bipolar disorder. Famous comedians Jim Carey has admitted to having it. Unfortunately, the late Robin Williams had a tremendous amount of depressive disorders that he came right out and told the public once he became famous in Hollywood to costars and directors at his early stardom in Hollywood. As a child, he was diagnosed with it and blamed it on being an only child.

Other notable celebrities are not new to the subject,but for those who follow them in the social media, you may very well know who they are.

Labels; Celebrities and non-labels

Therefore, label or no label, until he/she have been diagnosed with the disorder and mental conditions themselves, soberly, a doctor or someone labeling them as a bipolar or depressed person will only make things worse if he/she hasn't admitted to it.

For that matter, the one person should be tested or admit to the condition and be ready to admit that he/she has the disorder. With lots of treatment, counseling, and even an exercise / diet regimen, and the proper prescribed medication which has been prove to work through scientific studies, the debate on the subject matter can go on, especially in Hollywood. Hopefully, more celebrities will come out and admit to it while under treatment, as well as being sober, simultaneously. Learning more about it is a good start, as well as seeking medical advice and staying with it. It's a difficult thing to do, especially for celebrities, but naturally the first step is admittance.

# CHAPTER THREE ARE YOU BIPOLAR

The Complications of Bipolar Disorder

Bipolar disorder is a very common condition. Many people are afraid of seeking treatment because they believe that the condition is less common that it really is. Other people fail to recognize the symptoms of bipolar disorder in the people around them specifically because they underestimate the prevalence of bipolar disorder in the general population.

Recognizing the signs of bipolar disorder in people is sometimes difficult because of the very nature of the disorder. Bipolar disorder is characterized by a manic phase and a depressive phase. Some people with bipolar disorder might be diagnosed with depression. Other people with bipolar disorder might just go unnoticed in terms of their mental illness. However, learning to recognize the signs can help people with bipolar disorder get the help that they need.

Signs of Mania

People who are experiencing the mania associated with bipolar disorder can actually be the life of the party, and they can seem to be extremely energetic and productive in cases. Some people glamorize this behavior, which is one reason why this phase sometimes is not seen for what it is. However, people in the manic phase of bipolar disorder can be twitchy and anxious, feeling too jumpy to actually sit down and get their work completed. Other people in this situation can start to become too confident in their abilities and talents, which can cause all sorts of problems in their lives.

Some people in a severe manic phase may start to make a lot of impulsive decisions, getting into drugs, unprotected sexual intercourse, spending lots of money, or compulsively gambling. These people have so much surplus energy that they seem to be on fire, and their judgment is so compromised that they make decisions that can destroy their lives in the blink of an eye. Even some of the little things, like the fact that manic people tend to talk very quickly or tend to have a hard time sitting still, can be distressing for them on a regular basis.

Signs of Depression

The depressive phase of bipolar disorder is more recognizable. People who are in this phase soon lack all energy. They may spend a lot of their lives and their time sleeping. Concentrating, remembering things, and making decisions can be more difficult for them. Some people under-eat and some people overeat under these circumstances. People in this situation tend to separate themselves from everything, including families, friends, and activities that they used to love. Some depressives will become suicidal or entertain suicidal thoughts.

The striking contrast between the manic phase of bipolar disorder and the depressive phase can really throw people off, and this helps to make the entire condition so much more complicated. Some episodes will last hours. Some of them will last for months. Bipolar people are thrown into chaos on a regular basis. Fortunately, there are medications that can help them and it is possible to seek treatment. However, bipolar disorder needs to be seen as what it is.

# CHAPTER FOUR LIVING WITH BIPOLAR DISORDER

Everyone has mood swings from time to time, but what if your mood swings are hard to control? When you are bipolar your moods are unpredictable. Sometimes you may feel depressed and sometimes you may feel happy. Dealing with those different emotions can be challenging for a person with bipolar disorder to live a normal life. Learning to cope with your bipolar disorder is a challenge within itself, but with proper counseling and medication, you can live a healthy productive life.

What it's like to live with bipolar disorder

Living with bipolar disorder can be complicated. You not only have to manage your moods, but other everyday things may be difficult to do such as a taking care of your personal hygiene, keeping a job or going to school. Many people with bipolar disorder have a hard time doing those things and sometimes may need extra help to get things done.

When you have bipolar disorder sometimes if you are not careful you can lose the people around you. Keeping your cool during tough situations can be challenging and stressful when you are bipolar. You could wake up one morning and be depressed, or you can be so happy that you do things without thinking. Being bipolar can bring stress on your family and your friends. Dealing with a rapid cycle of mood swings can put a damper on your day to day life.

Taking your medication can make your life easier when you have bipolar disorder. The hardest thing about living with bipolar on a day to day basis is when the disorder is not treated. You can turn to drugs or alcohol like I mentioned to cope with your feelings of depression. You may say or do things that are out of the ordinary and ruin relationships. Living with bipolar disorder can be hard when you are trying to be in a romantic relationship. Sometimes people with bipolar disorder can become obsessive and angry. Managing those impulses on a day to day basis can take a toll on your mental health.

Not having a set schedule on a day to day basis can make your bipolar less manageable. Doing nothing with your life when you are bipolar can cause your mind to wander. You constantly have to deal with unwanted thoughts on a day to day basis. Sometimes those thoughts and feelings get overwhelming, and you may do things out of character.

Sometimes people with bipolar disorder attend day programs such as a partial hospital program. In these programs they learn social skills, coping skills and have a structured day. These programs can help people with bipolar disorder learn how to cope with their illness and add some excitement to their lives. It also gives people with bipolar disorder a chance to become friends with other people with the same illness.

People with bipolar disorder may deal with depression for an extended period of time. Bi means two, so sometimes you can feel elated and manic and other times you may feel like you do not want to live anymore. Usually going to therapy can help manage these emotions.

There is hope for people that have to live with bipolar disorder on a daily basis. With the proper medication, you can function just like other people. You can get a job, go to school and even be in a healthy relationship. The key to living with bipolar disorder is to take things slow. You don't want to take on too many responsibilities such as a working over time and taking too many classes at once.

Having friends and a support group can help you manage your bipolar symptoms. When you first get diagnosed with bipolar disorder, you can feel scared and alone. Although you have bipolar disorder, you can live a normal life. Doing day to day activities may take a little more effort. People with bipolar disorder can live well when they also have a schedule. Sticking to a schedule of when you take a shower, brush your teeth and clean your room can help make your day to day tasks easier. Bipolar disorder does not have to be a burden. The hardest reality is that you cannot get rid of bipolar disorder but with a little hope, you can easily learn how to manage it so you can enjoy your life.

# CHAPTER FIVE BIPOLAR TREATMENTS

Bipolar disorder is a psychological illness that causes the person to experience abnormal mood swings. People with bipolar disorder may experience episodes of depression and episodes of mania during which they may be irritable, impulsive, and euphoric. Due to the damaging effects of bipolar disorder, if left untreated, there is a need for ongoing research into the treatment for bipolar disorder. Bipolar disorder is a brain condition that results in wild shifts in mood, which have a negative impact on a person's ability to function at work and maintain stable relationships with friends and family. The mood swings can range from depression to mania. They can happen only a few times or several times. In certain cases, bipolar depression symptoms of depression and mania can happen at the same time. The disorder also has a tendency to be under diagnosed.

Some of the symptoms of bipolar disorder include abnormally elevated states (mania or hypomania) such as abnormally increased energy, decreased the need for sleep, reduced attention span, impaired judgment, substance abuse, and aggressive behavior. Effective bipolar disorder treatment can help manage the symptoms of the disorder even though there is no cure for bipolar disorder. Effective bipolar disorder treatment often includes medication, therapy, and lifestyle maintenance to manage this complex disorder.

Medication is perhaps the most important part of bipolar disorder treatment though many people including bipolar disorder patients do not take full advantage of the medication that is available. A psychiatrist often prescribes a mood stabilizing medication, however, bipolar disorder patients are notoriously inconsistent with taking their medication.

In addition to medication, psychotherapy is often recommended for bipolar disorder treatment. Therapy does not necessarily treat the bipolar disorder directly, but helps the individual cope with the symptoms and can help the person to learn to manage stress in order to reduce the bipolar disorder symptoms.

Relationships often suffer from bipolar disorder and its symptoms. Part of the therapeutic treatment for bipolar disorder can include family therapy, marriage counseling, or family sessions with the person's therapist to help strengthen the relationships and educate everyone on the effects of bipolar disorder.

Lifestyle management and regulation of self-care and habits are a common component of effective bipolar disorder treatment. It is strongly suggested that people with bipolar disorder maintain a regular sleep schedule and have a regular schedule of exercise and relaxation or stress management.

The general public has a lot of misconceptions about bipolar disorder. Therefore, the patient should educate themselves about bipolar disorder, its symptoms, and effective treatments. People with bipolar disorder may also have to educate their families and friends about the true nature of the disorder as opposed to the extreme cases of the unmanaged bipolar disorder that they may have heard in the media.

An important part of bipolar treatment is emotional support from friends and family. Not all bipolar disorder patients have supportive friends and family. If the patient has a lack of emotional support, they can seek support from stable resources such as support groups for bipolar disorder and depression.

Unfortunately, the bipolar disorder usually lasts an entire lifetime. Symptoms generally start to appear during teenage years. As of yet, there is no cure for this condition, and that is why there continues to be ongoing research into the treatment for bipolar disorder.

Bipolar disorder is typically treated with medication prescribed by a medical doctor, such as a psychiatrist. However, not every individual reacts to medications in the same way. Therefore, once diagnosed, the doctor may require the patient to maintain a journal of their daily activities, including details regarding their sleep patterns. This enables the doctor to develop a treatment regimen suited to the individual.

Mood stabilizing medications are the typical first line of offense against bipolar disorder once it is diagnosed. Lithium is one of the more common medications prescribed, and it was the first mood-stabilizing drug approved by the FDA for a treatment of mania. It is usually effective in controlling the symptoms of mania and in preventing the patient from slipping into depression.

It was also approved that valproic acid as an alternative to lithium in the treatment of bipolar disorder. In more recent years, anticonvulsant drugs such as lamotrigine have been employed as maintenance treatments for the condition. However, these anticonvulsant type drugs come with the warning to the effect that their use may increase the risk of suicide.

Atypical antipsychotic drugs such as risperidone and olanzapine, among others, are often used in acutely manic patients. These medications are typically prescribed in conjunction with another medication to assist in the maintenance of the disorder. These drugs are called atypical to set them apart from prior antipsychotic medications. Recently, it has been approved that olanzapine as a singular therapy for the maintenance of bipolar disorder.

Occasionally, antidepressant medications are also used as a treatment for bipolar disorder. Normally, this type of medication will be paired with a mood stabilizer. This is because of the increased risk of the patient switching to a mania or hypomania state when taking the antidepressant alone.

As with any type of medication, all of these medications used in the treatment for bipolar disorder have the potential for side effects. Drowsiness, headache, and nausea are common for all three types of medications used in the treatment.

Another form of treatment that may be employed in treating the disorder is psychotherapy. Psychotherapy provides guidance, education, and support to the patient being treated as well as their families. Psychotherapy may come in the form of cognitive behavioral therapy (CBT), which allows the patient to learn to make changes away from harmful thoughts and behaviors; family focused therapy which involves family members to act as a support group and to develop strategies for coping with the disorder; and such therapies as social rhythm therapy to help with relationships outside of the family and psycho education, which educates the patient all about the disorder.

Other treatments may include exercise, which is known to be effective in treating depression; omega 3 fatty acids; a ketogenic diet which is thought to help stabilize mood; and medical cannabis, although this is a more controversial treatment.

On going research seems to make consistent breakthroughs in the treatment for bipolar disorder. While there is still no cure for the condition, the treatments described previously to allow the patient to live a somewhat normal life.

# BOOK TWO
# DEPRESSION

## DEALING WITH DEPRESSION

By.
Leo Hardy

# CHAPTER ONE DEPRESSION AND THE FAMOUS

*-There is no fulfillment in things whatsoever. And I think one of the reasons that depression reigns supreme amongst the rich and famous is some of them thought that maybe those things would bring them happiness. But what, in fact, does is having a cause, having a passion. And that's really what gives life's true meaning. -Ben Carson*

Depression is a serious mental health issue. This illness can happen to any person at any time. People become sad and hopeless. Anyone can become depressed regardless of age, gender, socioeconomic status, and race. Famous people such as actors, actresses, and singers have suffered from depression. Money doesn't buy happiness all the time. These are some famous people that have had battles with depression.

Jon Hamm

At the age of 20 Hamm suffered from a serious episode of depression. After his father died he became depressed. He said that a structured environment kept him busy and helped him break out of it. He was in college and working at the time. He also attended therapy sessions and used antidepressants at this time. It took him some time but he was able to break away from the depression and get out of bed. He went on to have a successful career.

Ashley Judd

Judd has a great career today, a loving family, and does humanitarian work to help give back. Things were not always good for her. When she was in sixth grade she was depressed and considered suicide to end it all. She got so bad that she went to a rehab clinic and stayed there for 42 days. She said that the clinic saved her and taught how her to handle life situations. She was able to reconnect with her family. She also found that helping others through charity work has helped. She was able to make peace with her past and bring something positive into her life.

Owen Wilson

To those that look at Wilson now it seems like he is pretty laid back. In 2007 Wilson was so depressed that he attempted suicide. In addition to depression he had issues with drug abuse that made his depression worse. Wilson sought help for his troubles. He got clean and stopped using drugs. He also spent time with friends and family to help bring him out of his depression.

Heath Ledger

Heath was a star that did not survive his depression. He overdosed on a mixture of sleeping pills, pain killers, and anxiety medication. After he died it became public that he suffered from depression for a number of years. Due to his depression and reckless behavior he lost his wife and she took custody of their daughter. Heath was a tragic loss due to depression and the feeling of hopelessness.

Demi Lovoto

This singer and actress had a very public experience with depression. In 2010 things got so bad that she checked herself into a treatment facility to help her deal with emotional and physical issues. She did this to get her life under control. While she was suffering from depression she was also suffering from anorexia, bulimia, and she found out that she has bipolar disorder. She went through manic periods and now with the correct treatment she has her life under control.

David Arquette

After splitting from his wife in 2010 David went through a time of depression. He was drinking often and exhibiting some reckless behavior. David went to a treatment facility to deal with his depression as well as his alcohol use. He got sober in treatment and learned coping skills. He also go more in touch with his emotions and learned to express them in a healthy manner.

Catherine Zeta Jones

This actress has a loving husband , a great career, and she is beautiful. She also suffers from bipolar II and severe depression. Since her diagnosis she has found ways to deal with life and improve her mental health. She is sharing her story with the world in hopes to help others.

Andre Waters

Waters was a football player in the NFL. Many people including his family and fans were surprised when he committed suicide in 2006. It turned out he was suffering from depression and brain damage that may have been caused by concussions from playing football. Those close to him say that his feeling of sadness would not go away and he took his life in order to escape it.

Gwyneth Paltrow

This actress seemed to have it all. After having her son she reported that she was not able to access her emotions. It turned out that she was suffering from postpartum depression. Many people think that women with this depression cry everyday and are not able to care for their child. There are many different depths of this depression. Paltrow was able to get help and her life back on track.

Princess Diana

Even though she was Royalty Diana suffered from depression. She was left alone when she married into this well known family. After she had her children she also suffered from postpartum depression. As her marriage fell apart she became more depressed. The family did little to help with her emotional well being. It took many years to overcome this depression. Diana also got involved in charity work and giving back to others had also helped her move on.

Robin Williams

For years this funny man had a dark side that no too many people knew about. He had a deep struggle with depression. Things got so hopeless for him that Robin ended up taking his own life. He struggled for many years and people did not realize how sad he was until it was too late.

Tipper Gore

The former first lady came forward that she was suffering from depression and had gone to treatment. She also took medication for a period of time to help with the depression. She realized that she needed help and could not shake the hopeless feeling on her own. She went public to try to help others that are suffering.

Marilyn Monroe

-It's better to be unhappy alone than unhappy with someone - so far. – Marilyn Monroe

Born June 1 1926 and died on August 5 1962

She was the most iconic star of the twentieth century. Considered by many the most beautiful woman on earth she battled depression for years before her death. A death that was ruled a probable suicide.

Depression can happen to anyone. These famous people may have the money and many fans but it does not mean they are immune to depression. When a person is experiencing signs of depression it is important they seek treatment right away. There are a number of different methods to help with depression and a person will not have to go through life with a feeling of hopelessness.

# CHAPTER TWO WHAT IS DEPRESSION

*- Depression has been called the world's number one public health problem. In fact, depression is so widespread it is considered the common cold of psychiatric disturbances. But there is a grim difference between depression and a cold. Depression can kill you. - David D. Burns*

Depression is a serious mental illness that can have debilitating effects on those who suffer from it. The illness can affect virtually anyone—adolescents, adults, and even the elderly. Depression is caused by a chemical imbalance in the brain, as well as other factors, and it is known to cause sadness, loss of interest, irregular sleep patterns, and strained relationships with loved ones. Despite the fact that depression is a complicated illness, there are treatments available.

Scientists generally agree that there are several chemicals in the brain that play a role in depression. These chemicals are related to mood, and they include serotonin, dopamine, and norepinephrine. Basically, during a depressive episode, these chemicals are lower than they should be. If left unchecked, abnormally low levels of these brain chemicals can lead to the aforementioned effects of depression.

It is important to remember that the causes of depression aren't limited to chemical factors. Loss, financial trouble, and even gender-specific experiences can cause depression. When someone experiences loss, they often find themselves feeling empty. Strong feelings of emptiness after a loss can be a sign of depression.

Furthermore, obsessing over the loss can be unhealthy and lead to depression as well.

Financial trouble has caused many people to become depressed. People worry that they won't be able to support themselves and / or their families, for example. Financial trouble can be especially depressing for people who are used to contributing heavily to the financial well-being of their family. In this case, these sorts of people may see themselves as a failure or a let-down to their family. This can be depressing in itself.

Gender-specific experiences can be related to life events like a pregnancy. Some women feel depressed after a pregnancy, and the depression has been reported to last up to several years for some women. In men, low testosterone levels can lead to depression. This occurs primarily later in life, which explains why some older men experience depression.

Depression has many causes, and it also has a multitude of effects. One of the most well-known effects of depression is sadness. People with depression often feel sad, dejected, hopeless, etc. With depression, these feelings can be long-lasting and severe. There is a difference between someone who experiences a financial loss, is sad for a few days, and then returns to normal and someone who experiences a financial loss and is sad for many months.

Along with sadness comes withdrawal from normal activities. Depression individuals often choose not to engage in the activities that they formerly enjoyed. They may quit their job, stop seeing friends and family, stop going to community activities, etc. This withdrawal from normal activities can actually worsen depression, as the depressed individual begins to feel more and more alone.

Loss of interest is related to withdrawal from normal activities, and it is another effect of depression. Those who are depressed may withdraw from an activity because they don't want others to see the state that they are in, but they also may withdraw from the activity because they feel that they have genuinely lost interest in the activity. For example, imagine someone named John who loves to paint. John may withdraw from painting if he becomes depressed, and he may do this because he feels that painting isn't interesting anymore.

Irregular sleep patterns are also an effect of depression. In particular, people who are depressed may find themselves sleeping much more than they used to. Some depressed individuals may feel that they need the extra sleep because they are very tired, while others may sleep just so that they don't have to deal with the challenges of everyday life.

Depression affects the person who is depressed in another way as well—it strains relationships with loved ones. Loved ones try to make the person feel better, but sometimes this can prove to be an impossible task. Furthermore, the depressed individual may act as though he doesn't care about his loved ones anymore, even though he does. Loved ones often try different things to help the depressed person cope, but sometimes these are met with failure. All of these different factors strain the relationships that the depressed person has, and the depressed individual may end up becoming alienated because of his illness.

An essential part of understanding depression is being aware of different treatment options. There are psychiatrists, psychologists, and other mental health professionals that can assist the patient in different ways. Psychiatrists focus on providing drugs, known as anti-depressants. These drugs address the aforementioned chemical causes of depression, such as low serotonin. Antidepressants can increase the level of serotonin and bring it up to normal. They can also increase the other brain chemicals associated with depression.

Psychologists have a degree in psychology, but that is different from psychiatrists. Psychiatrists have a medical degree. Psychologists rely on talk therapy, one example being cognitive behavioral therapy. In this type of therapy, the psychologist addresses negative thinking patterns that the patient has become accustomed to. After bringing these negative patterns to light, the psychologist suggests new types of positive thinking patterns. This type of therapy helps patients learn to address the part of depression that they have control over—their thoughts.

Sometimes, a combination approach is used to treat depression. This can involve a patient seeing a psychiatrist and a psychologist in order to obtain medication and therapy, respectively. Combination approaches can be particularly effective because they target the multiple causes of depression. As a quick reminder, depression is caused by biological factors (i.e. an imbalance of mental chemicals), but it is also caused by other factors that have already been discussed.

Depression is complex, and it is often necessary to try multiple approaches to treat the illness. Each individual requires his or her own, unique treatment plan. It is key for depressed individuals to stay involved with friends, family, and activities they enjoy. Doing these things will help alleviate depression, even if doing them is challenging. The first step to dealing with depression is understanding it.

# CHAPTER THREE THE SIGNS OF DEPRESSION

Depression can be defined as having an impended doomed feeling, lifeless and apathetic. It varies from one person to the other. Depressed men feel restless and angry. Depression is different from normal sadness because it engulfs the daily life of a person are different signs that can make one know that a person is suffering from depression The signs can persist for a couple of weeks or months and may interfere with the daily life of the person. It occurs gradually to some people hence difficult to notice.

Doctors describe depression as mild, moderate, severe or sub threshold. A person is described to have a mild depression when it has impacted his/her daily life. Moderate depression is when has a significant impact on someone's life hence making it difficult for him/her to get on with the daily operations. People with depression have psychotic symptoms. On the other hand, subthreshold depression is where a person has fewer than 5 depression symptoms.This syndrome can cause distress. If this kind of depression lasts for some years, the condition is called dysthymia.

Depression can also be grouped into postnatal depression, bipolar depression and seasonal effective disorder. Some women develop depression after conceiving. This is termed as postnatal depression. And can be treated in the similar way as the as the other depression. Therapies and medicine are a perfect solution for this kind of depression. The signs of depression may emerge inform of feelings, behaviors, thoughts and through physical responses. One is unable to concentrate on the daily activities

.Some other people may withdraw from close friends and relatives. The following are the common signs of depression:

Changed feelings

Depression is a disease that affect everyone. Major depression is a disorder that affect the way one feels about life. Many depressed people develop a hopeless outlook on life. This is a common sign that helps a lot to know when a person who is close to you is suffering from depression. Other people develop a feeling of self-hate and inappropriate guilt. The common reoccurring thoughts of depression can be focalized as the depressed person's fault.

Anxiety and irritability

Depressed people fee down and not shaking. The things that had been making them happy becomes of no interest to them. The physical and mental toll of depression contributes to irritability and anxiety. In most cases depression affects sexes in different ways. According to the research, men who are irritable because of depression display signs that have no association with depression i.e. escapist, substance abuse and misplaced anger.

Changes on their appetite.

Some depressed people may gain weight while other can lose it. An increase in appetite is possibly the reason of gaining weight. Other people loss appetite hence losing weight in a tremendous way.

Slow thinking, speaking and body movement

Depressed people become slow thinkers and always take a longer time to speaker a single sentence. Some can even experience slow movements.

Frequent thoughts of death

This is a serious sign of depression. This is where it becomes prominent when one begin to think about ending his/her life. This is where one feels that he/she is a failure or worthless in life. Some fells that other people will be better off without them.

# CHAPTER FOUR The great depression ended So will yours

It can be difficult when you are suffering from depression to see an end in sight. But one nice thing about recovery in this modern age is that medical science has very effective treatments for depression. You might feel that it is hard to entrust your health to others, but you are in good hands.

Depression is a disease caused by a chemical imbalance in the brain. The neurotransmitters that make you happy, such as dopamine, serotonin, and norepinephrine, are not at their proper levels in between the synapses. This causes the brain to lack the chemicals necessary for positive reactions to life events. And it also means that you have less energy than ever during the day, because you don't have any motivation to react to positive stimuli in your environment. You will probably feel that nothing is worth doing anymore, that you don't want to see anyone, and that your life is not worth living.

Thankfully, these feelings are temporary. This is just a progression of depression, not your actual usual outlook on life. You are probably usually chattier, happier, and in general more of a go getter with your tasks. You may be tempted to worry that you will always feel this way, and that you are irreparably broken. This is a fallacy however, and with time and treatment, your chemicals will be back to normal, or better than normal.

Depression treatments are the most difficult part. If the depression is mostly chemical, then don't expect to feel any better until a month on the medication. This might sound like a lot of time, but some people go for years with untreated depression. Really, in the long scheme of things, a month isn't that long to wait. However, if after a month your medication is not working, your doctor might switch meds or add in something else to help boost the medication's effects. Sometimes people even report feeling worse before they feel better, and that is completely normal.

Oftentimes, this treatment time is a blessing in disguise if you have a more serious ailment. A lot of times people who thought they have depression really end up being diagnosed with bipolar disorder. This mood ailment is very severe at times, so it is important to get the mood swings from mania to depression under control before another, possibly more serious, episode occurs.

You might notice the drugs are kicking in, and you actually feel emotionally dislodged. This is probably because you need to deal with the psychological side that an illness like depression presents in order to make a full recovery. Health is quite a multi-faceted state of being, and people with depression might have ignored their emotional health for a while. Now, they are awakening again, and ready to deal with some of the regrets and hurts from the past in more proactive ways than they previously have. And you might be one of those people that needs to find new tools for coping with stress and challenges in life. And that is alright, because those new tools a therapist can give you will only make you a stronger, more resilient person.

When you feel like there is no light at the end of the tunnel, recognize that that is a lie that your brain is telling you right now. You don't feel good, so it's normal to have darker thoughts. But try to listen to people who know that you will be okay with time and help. And when it feels like forever, go back to self soothing behaviors that worked for you in the past to cope with your depression. Recovery is possible, but the way you have been doing things in the past might have been more of a bandage than a medicine. Both of those things are good, because you need to self soothe. But you also want to take the help being offered to you so that you do not have to return to such a dark place in life again. The good thing is that once depression is treated, you can have your life back again. And functioning might be difficult, but it will be a manageable sort of difficult. You can have the peace of mind right now that it will get better.

# CHAPTER FIVE The Emotional Aspects of Depression

Depression is a challenging mental illness to deal with on a daily basis. It can cause feelings of sadness, make the depressed individual more withdrawn, cause the individual to have a loss of interest in activities that he formerly found enjoyable, and can even lead to suicidal thoughts and actions. When thinking about depression, it is important to understand how grief and loss play a role. Losing a loved one is a great emotional blow, and the grieving process can often be arduous.

The loss of a person that someone was close to causes depression in several ways. First, there is the realization that one will never see the lost individual again. There will be no more happy memories, no more bonding, etc. This alone can cause someone to experience depression. People who become depressed due to loss often were very close with the person who has passed away. Furthermore, the depressed individual may have had a close relationship with the person who passed on. All of these factors contribute to depression.

The loss of a loved one can also cause depression due to the fact that one's daily routine changes substantially. Consider the husband and wife who are married for thirty years when one of them suddenly passes away. How will the other go about their day without the company of their spouse? Simple things like going out to eat can bring back memories of the deceased, and this can be a painful experience for the person who has experienced a loss.

Loss is definitely not easy to experience, but grieving can be equally trying. The grieving process consists of several stages, and these can vary depending on who you ask. Regardless of the specific steps, grieving can involve some general experiences, such as thinking about all of the reasons why someone was special, hoping the deceased is in a better place, cherishing memories, and recovery. This last step is important—at the end of a grieving process, one should be able to recover from the loss they experienced. They should be able to resume their daily activities, engage with friends and family, and go back to work. However, many people struggle with recovery and, instead of recovering, they become depressed. People who become depressed often focus solely on the fact that the deceased will never be in their life again, instead of concentrating on the good things that the deceased did in their life, or the fact that they are in a better place now.

When a person who has experienced a loss becomes depressed as a result of their grief, it is time to see a mental health professional. There are several types of mental health professionals that the person should consider—psychologists, psychiatrists, therapists, and even life coaches (as long as they are reputable). Seeing one of these professionals can help alleviate the negative feelings associated with grief and loss, and can help the person return to their normal life. If the person neglects to see a mental health professional, he may become more and more depressed as he focuses on the negativity associated with grief and loss. In some cases, it is even necessary for friends and family to motivate someone to see a mental health professional.

Once the patient and the mental health professional connect, the patient's depression can be treated in a variety of ways. Psychiatrists prescribe anti-depressants, while psychologists and other professionals use different methods of talk therapy to help the patient improve his mental state. Through talking to the patient, the mental health professional may be able to change the patient's cognition, also known as the way he thinks about things. In other words, the professional would help the patient think about loss and grief in a more positive light. Additionally, a patient who formerly dwelled on the negative aspects of loss may be able to learn new ways of coping by talking with a mental health professional.

Therapy can achieve strong positive results, but this is not to discount medication. Sometimes, therapy is more effective when combined with the right medication. It may take some time and some experimentation with different medicines and different types of therapy, but most people who experience a loss are eventually able to recover and return to their daily lives. This is not to say that they have forgotten about the person they lost. In fact, it is often quite the opposite. The person who experienced a loss understands that the deceased will not return to this world, but he is able to keep the person alive through positive thoughts and memories.

# CHAPTER SIX The Road Back From Depression

Depression is treatment can be full of up's and down's, just like the actual illness. However, you can be assured that once you are on the path to treating your depression, and if you stay on that path, that you will be better off than before.

When you leave your depression untreated, it can actually cause you to miss out on a lot of life. And there is also the fact that untreated depression is actually damaging to your brain, while medicine can help regenerate those underutilized neural pathways. This is why you are not being tough by ignoring your depression; you could just be making yourself really sick. It's hard for people to get treatment because there is a stigma regarding mental illness. But it shouldn't be there, because if you know you aren't feeling good, then there is a path to recovery awaiting. Some people have gotten so used to being sick that they don't even remember what it is like to live depression free. But there is a way to regain your health through treatment, so you don't need to stay in the shadows.

When you take medicine for depression, you are boosting the neurotransmitters that your brain needs to be content and derive pleasure from stimuli. You might take antidepressants, which are probably the most popular treatment for depression. There are different categories of these medications, such as tricyclics, monoamine oxidase inhibitors (MAOI's), and serotonin reuptake inhibitors. Each of these subsets of pills has different effects on the neurotransmitters.

One reason people might not choose the older group of antidepressants, MAOI's, is that these pills do not mix well with many foods. In fact, it can be dangerous to eat certain cheeses with them, as well as other foods on the prohibited list. People with depression are already not feeling that good, and probably do not want to spend what little energy they have blacklisting food. They might be so depressed that they cannot even follow the doctor's' instructions. This is why these pills are now underutilized.

The tricyclics are new, and a lot of them have effect on norepinephrine. That is why people like to take these pills if they are feeling sleepy due to their depression. It gives them a bit of a boost to react to things with more energy. Some tricyclics are popular, like Wellbutrin, for their antimanic properties. They can be given to a patient who might be bipolar, and the patient will probably not have a manic reaction. Wellbutrin is also very popular because it does not cause the patient to generally gain weight and does not tend to have any sexual side effects, such as loss of libido.

Serotonin Reuptake Inhibitors (SSRI's) are very well respected because they actually have a strong effect on depression. Prozac in particular is an older drug and has been quite effective in many cases throughout the years. One of the reasons it's so popular is because a person can take a high dose, up to 60mgs a day. This means that the doctor can keep upping the dose until the patient feels real relief from the depression symptoms. SSRI's are not without their complications. Many people suffer from weight gain and sexual side effects from taking these drugs. That is why they might be reluctant to try them. However, untreated depression also has effects on weight and libido, so it is a bit of a catch 22. It is much better to give yourself a chance to feel better, and the SSRI's are quite mild compared to some of the alternatives for depression.

When a person has unipolar depression or depression with a psychotic episode, very often an antipsychotic is added to the mix. The antipsychotic might be added for around 6 months to two years to help the person to stabilize. Psychotic episodes are very hard on the brain and are thought to be caused by too much dopamine flooding the back of the brain, causing auditory hallucinations and delusions. Sometimes if a person is really sick, they will experience visual hallucinations as well. Antipsychotics like Rexulti might be added to an antidepressant to boost the effect of the pill and help the patient feel better quickly. However, this is mainly in treatment resistant patients or patients struggling with suicidal tendencies.

People with bipolar depression will be put on a mood stabilizer. This is the staple of bipolar treatment, the most prominent choice being lithium. Lithium is called the gold standard treatment for bipolar, but it can be very hard on the kidneys and the thyroid in long term use. Usually the person is monitored closely with regular blood work to ensure that the treatment is not having a damaging effect.

Another treatment for treatment resistant depression is electroshock therapy. This is actually very effective in stimulating the brain's serotonin production and release. However, some people suffer memory problems after the treatment, which are more than likely temporary, but scary for the person at the time. In rare cases, people complain of permanent loss of memory, however it is not likely that this is actually from the shock therapy.

People coming out of depression like to access counselling. It is important for patients to be aware that depression has taken some time from their lives where they could have been growing and producing. They might feel a sense of grief or loss over that time, and their emotional, which depression blunts, can come back stronger than ever after this period. They might find comfort in group therapy where other members open up about their experience with mental illness. Or, you as a patient could choose a psychologist to work through the issues one on one. Psychology is a good investment of your time, but it can also be expensive. That is why it is good to visit the psychologist once the pain has started to subside a bit from the actual illness of depression. When you think that you are just left with emotional scars, then counseling can help heal those.

There is a road to recovery with depression that can be dealt with nicely in the healthcare system. Try to be open to the possibility that life after depression might look a little different, but it may be healthier and more fulfilling as well.

# CHAPTER SEVEN DEPRESSION AFFECTS WOMEN AND MEN DIFFERENTLY

We all find ourselves in a stressful situation at one point or another. We tend to get overwhelmed with work and responsibilities adding stress to our lives. Stress is simply a part of life since we deal with different things every day. However, if stress is not well managed, it can lead to more serious issues such as depression. Research indicates that women deal with stress differently than men. Mostly, when women are stressed, they look for emotional support from friends and families. They also take care of those who are close to them. Below are several ways that women and men deal with stress.

Hormones play a significant role in determining how people deal with stress. When a woman is under stress, her body releases the stress hormone that prepares the body for fight or flight. She also produces a hormone called Oxytocin that is usually connected with the maternal feeling, breastfeeding and loving feeling. Oxytocin enhances relaxation, lower stress response and reduces fearfulness. The woman also produces estrogen hormone that amplifies the effects of oxytocin.

Women tend to respond to stress by offering protection to themselves and their friends through nurturing them. They also join a social group so she can create friends that she can talk to. When a woman is faced with a challenging or stressful situation, she tends to look for someone she can lean on and talk about her problems.

On the other hand, men produce less oxytocin hormones as compared to women. And when faced with stress, they try to keep to themselves or run away from the problem. The male hormones usually lessen the effect of oxytocin. The study indicates that men are the most likely fight or run away from the situation.

When men are stressed, in most times, they don't prefer to talk to anyone, but instead, they keep to themselves. One of the primary reason why men are reluctant to look or health from a specialist is because they don't want to be seen as a counselor or a therapist. They do not want to appear weak and want to show others he is capable of handling problems on their own.

# CHAPTER EIGHT DEPRESSION AND BIOCHEMISTRY

Some say that depression is a chemical imbalance and not a "real" disease. Others state that It is an illness that affects your brain. This can be a serious illness that is caused by changes in your brain chemistry. The onset can be caused by other factors like changes in hormone levels, stress, difficult life circumstances, genetics, or certain medical conditions. This is not only a serious condition but also a common one. Depression is one of The most disabling disorders worldwide according to The World Health Organization. In The United States, approximately twelve percent of men and twenty-one percent of women have an incident of depression at some time in their lifetime.

Depression can affect anyone regardless of age, gender, ethnic group, or race. One big problem with this condition is problems It can cause are often made worse that many suffering from depression are never diagnosed or treated. When identified quickly and treated symptoms can be manageable. This condition can be treated with prescription medications like antidepressants but if you do not want to take medications or your case is a mild one there are other treatments that you can try first.

You can try to reduce your stress levels by using yoga and meditation daily, making lifestyle changes in your eating habits and sleeping, exercising, and listening to relaxing music. Other non-medicine treatments you can use include:

• Doing aerobic exercises is one effectual way of treating depression. Other exercises you can use are a thirty-minute walk, swimming, biking, or any activity that will get your heart rate up to help release mood-boosting endorphins in your brain.• Get plenty of sunshine and during wintertime when days are shorter take a vitamin D tablet. Spending just ten minutes of sun daily can help improve your mood• Make sure that you are getting at least eight hours of sleep a night.• Eat foods like fruits and vegetables, whole grains, and get enough protein every day. Try to stay away from caffeine and refined sugars as they could contribute to feelings of depression and anxiety.• Start a journal and write down your feelings and thoughts every day.• Spend quality time with family and friends.

If your symptoms do not seem to be improving or are getting worse talk to your physician. Your episodes could be a symptom of a medical condition. Once that medical condition is treated, your symptoms should decrease. You can make an appointment with a psychiatrist or psychologist to talk about things that could be bothering you like starting a new job, ending a marriage, or other things.

# CHAPTER NINE MEDICAL TREATMENT

There are many classifications of medication that can be used to treat this condition. Each classification has their side effects and positives. Depression medications that are used for treatments alter the neurotransmitters, (chemical messengers) in your brain. Normally it can take four to eight weeks for you to feel the total effects of the medications. Most will need to continue the antidepressant medicine for six to twelve months or longer. There is no single medicine that is the best treatment. Generally forty to sixty percent of patients have a positive response to the first medication they are put on.

Selective Serotonin Reuptake Inhibitors (SSRIs)

• Lexapro• Paxil, Pexeva, Paxil CR• Celexa• Zoloft• Prozac, Prozac Weekly

Common side effects

• Sexual problems• Insomnia• Anxiety, nervousness• Headache• Dizziness• Possible weight gain• Diarrhea• Stomach upset• Constipation• Sweating

Positives

• Less weight gain is noticed with Celexa, Prozac. Prozac Weekly, and Zoloft• Prozac and Prozac Weekly have a lower rate of withdrawal symptoms

Serotonin-Norepinephrine Reuptake Inhibitors

• Venlafaxine• Effexor XR• Khedezia• Cymbalta• Pristiq

Common side effects

• Dry mouth• Drowsiness, insomnia• Nausea• Dizziness• Sexual problems• Sweating• Anxiety• Headaches

Positives

• Once-a day-dosing with most of these• Venlafaxine is slightly more effective in resistant or refractory depression

Other antidepressants

• Remeron, Remeron Sol Tab• Vibryd• Wellbutrin, Wellbutrin SR, Wellbutrin XL, Budeprion SR, Forfivo XL, Aplenzin• Serzone• Oleptro

Common side effects

• Headache• Dry mouth• Nausea• Weight loss or gain• Diarrhea or constipation• Insomnia or drowsiness• Abnormal dreams• Sweating• Confusion or agitation• Dizziness

Positives

• Bupropion can be associated with modest weight loss• Olepto, Serzone, and Bupropion are not as likely to cause sexual dysfunction• For patients who are depressed and feel fatigued or lethargic may find taking Bupropion helpful• If you have trouble sleeping that is associated with depression taking Serzone, Oleptro, Remeron, or Remeron SolTab• Remeron SolTab, Remeron may have a faster onset of action.

In conclusion, to truly understand all of the possible treatments that are available you should consult a medical professional. Keep in mind that overcoming depression will not be easy, but it is possible. Millions of people have walked this road and so can you.

## Don't miss out!

Click the button below and you can sign up to receive emails whenever Leo Hardy publishes a new book. There's no charge and no obligation.

Sign Me Up!

https://books2read.com/r/B-A-TYTD-CZLN

BOOKS 2 READ

Connecting independent readers to independent writers.

www.ingramcontent.com/pod-product-compliance
Lightning Source LLC
Chambersburg PA
CBHW071258280526
45788CB00004B/1757

* 9 7 8 1 5 4 5 5 7 3 5 6 3 *